Insane Times

Insane Times

Font Interior:: Garamond
Font Cover:: Delphi SF
Design and Cover: Nadia Khan
Other books by the writer:
Emron, the Unknown Hero
Life Water
Once Again

ISBN-13: 978-91-86173-05-0

Insane Times

Ejaz Khan

Insane Times

To poetry lovers!

Insane Times

A tiny drop

A tiny drop couldn't stand the heat
When touched by the flame of love
The body shattered, essence was freed
The joyful dance with weightless steps
It takes its flight, towards the heavens above
To touch the flame of love

In frenzy of quest, with untiring zeal
It went on climbing high
And joined the ranks of alike
The liberated drops in sway
Singing, dancing, all the way
What a feeling! To be finally free
The hearts trembling with excitement immense

The tiny drop's consciousness expanded
It felt strong, invincible
It looked down and saw the Earth beneath
It looked up and saw the limitless sky
And felt split
The indecision made it weak
It shivered and shrank
In the freezing cold
No longer, determined and bold

The Earth dragged it down
The flame pulled it up
And it felt torn apart
It cried in pain
Turn all a tear
And fell on the thirsty land

A Toy

Alluring, self-absorbed
Perfidious, conceited
Deprived of candor
An insignificant drop
In a boundless ocean
Ignorant of the fact
Out there in realm of deceit
He's nothing
But a puppet on a string
Just a toy
In hands of gods
All fragile, all vulnerable
With free will or without
As the true meanings
Of principle divine
Remain hidden from his perception

****

A Time to come!

Not so long ago
There was a readiness to pay
To get access to poets deep thoughts
But time changed and there're left
No poetry lovers but poets
Who'll give favors to each other
To read the works, extracts of mind
That time is not far away
When a poet has to pay
In order to be read

****

A simple truth

Not all your thoughts are beautiful
Not all you say is great
Anyone, who says otherwise
Certainly is a fawner or a hypocrite

A vicious circle

A starting point full of promise
An obvious end, a goal to achieve
Darkness, all embracing
Feathers exposed to raging storms
Endless struggle
Against all odds
Relations so unreliable
Events so unpredictable
A bumpy, thorny path
Stretching from hell to hell
Surrounded by ravines
Forlorn heart falls victim
When passions and desires unfold
Shadows enslave
Dragging deeper and deeper
In quagmires of materialism
A Warlord's claim

The warlord rode uphill
Looked down with pride
Pointed towards the east
And said in an arrogant way
To his impressed guests
I own all the land
As far as you can spot
Earth beneath his feet
Shook with a great rumble
Was it laughter or a grumble
No one could say for sure
As no-one heard her say
You haughty fool

I was there
From time immemorial
Long before you were even conceived
And I'll be, long after you're gone
Why are you so totally deceived
These six feet of you
Belong to dust of mine
And not the other way around

*****

A warrior's way

You ought to alienate
Fears that entangle
Attach no value to grieves
Hold tight to strong beliefs
Said the one in sack clothes

Mishaps are but part of existence
Strife is the price for attainments
Be like warriors great
Who fight, struggle, on any rate
Be patient and wait!
For the caller to call
Life's but full of negation
Accept even below expectation

Remember, at times lay open
The escape-routes, so that you may flee
At others you're forced
To take a firm stand
Choose the moment of action
Prudently, wisely
Hold the secret tight
As you stand and fight
There exist no sanctuaries
Neither in state of vigilance
Nor in colorful dreams
The joy is but time-bound
Reflecting, vanishing
In dimensions unknown
As if it was a mirage

Pains n sufferings aren't any exceptions
They too are unable to last for long
Then why to sob or scream?

******

Credit goes to…

Thousands of hands were involved
Some visible some unseen
From architect to painter
Plumber, carpenter and all the rest
Displayed their craftsmanship
Creating a comfortable, beautiful house
When the building finally stood ready
It was proudly pronounced
Mr. X had built a house
The man, who never had put his foot there
Till the house was all complete

A wind of change

The world flutters in the iron grip
Changes too abrupt, too harsh, pain overwhelming
Greed, devouring the sky high green
The great habitats of species diverse
The experimental labs of evolving life
The pulse irregular, the heartbeat frail
The light of conscience dim, the mind paralyzed
From south to north it blows
Making arctic ices to shrink
Forcing glaciers to recede
Melting drop by drop they become
What they really were

Deep down, the furnaces aglow
Preparing a great shudder, a serious blow
Oceans lament, as squander keeps replacing
The wondrous, thriving life
The contaminated air struggles to get a fresh

Turmoil, chaos twirls around
Invoking the hells to descend
On the face of Earth
As insanity, the new plague
Keeps haunting, taking its toll
As the nature seems to have enough

LOVE

Love is the power, most potent
Equally valid and in demand everywhere
Ever striving for more, never ever content
Unlimited, ready to go to any extent.
Seeking ruthlessly the opportunities to consume itself
On objects it holds dear
At times it is blind, at times sees crystal clear
It can pierce the sky like a shooting star
Ready to jump in the bottomless pit
All the heavenly bodies are lit by it
It can make you fearless or make you tremble in the
heart
It can make you whole or tear you apart
It expresses itself through uncountable mediums and
shapes.
In ever changing ways
In darkness you'll find it, though clothed in golden
rays
By the power of its magnetic pull
The opposite poles get closer without knowing why
Thus emerge the worlds new

The process of creation and recreation is only
possible
Due to this mysterious force.
All the forms of life spring from this force potent.
The worlds' would disintegrate and perish
If the playful love is gone

A revelation

Knock, knock
Who's there?
Me! Your maker
Go away, I'm bitter
I won't open my heart
You fool!
It's from there I knock!
Why you keep looking
Out in space

*****

A caution

Don't evoke the power you can't control
The law of nature states
That the stronger dominates
And destroys the weaker
When it resists
Though the law exempts
If driven and functioning under the principles
Of compassion and love

A microcosm

A wonder that's a body
Home of thriving life
A grand story of miracle at work
A perpetual drama of life and death
Seen and lived by
From the angle of
A tiny, insignificant cell
That lives a fleeting life
Centre of power, the throbbing heart
From the lowest points
To the centre high
All abide by the law
Assigned functions
Perfect order, no defying
A journey unending
Each muscle, each thread of nerve
A mystery profound
Each vein, each gut
Tells the story of
A constant orbiting
A never ending flow
Vital energy, reaching all
The well being of the body secured
What a wonderful lesson
Only if one could see
And implement the same principles
Outside the confinement of microcosm
Once the order fails
Chaos enters
Destroys the balances delicate
The bodies crumble
Both in microcosms and macrocosm

A million ways to live

Millions paths emerge
Out from passage of time
Each moment presents
Task small or big
Offering solutions diverse
Events take place
Inviting to lefts and rights
Opportunities appear and disappear
As if just a mirage
Life goes on
Following the wavy trails
A million ways to live
A million ways to die
Suspended in between
A tiny, vibrant life
Fears for choices, poor
Torn by sorrows and regrets
As none knows the art
To make the decisions correct
Each moment offers an occasion
To select, to gamble
A game of hazard
Where all are ultimate losers
Except for fate
The only winner
A fact well conceived
But rather too late

A womb eternal

Appointed time for everything
A long journey stretching
From cradle to last resting place
A time to laugh, a moment to cry
Thousand desires, needs to satisfy
Love, hate and all the other emotions
Valor, cowardice and all the rights and wrongs
Strange invading notions
Inhabit mind
Destination appears and disappears
Like mirage in bemused, hazy landscape
Where static time looks bewildered
As life passes by
Incidents and accidents
Occurring in succession
Creating a strange, magical junction
Where time and space turn
Variables interchangeable
Train of life passing through
Life and not time is, mother of all

*****

Calm before the storm

Calm before the storms
Dance before the doom
Dim luster of the stars
Shakes earth beneath my feet
Sound spread the beat of drums
Mars demands the field of war

All angels of apocalypse
With all the calamities in store
Rush around and seal
All the ways of flight
While wicked hearts go blind
Closing the doors of perception

The heartbeat of the Earth sinks
Before it gets faster out of stress
Fearing the dreadful day
Wishing its inhabitants to wake up and pray
But ears of the race remained deaf
Transgressing, arrogantly defying

So brilliantly shines the glory
So perfect's the day
Looking around with bewildered eyes
The souls of pious go astray
Heart and mind create confusion
When bodily senses betray

Hear you too, the sound of nearing steps?

Dark Shadows

Pushing forward to attain the levels high
Breaking the age old patterns
Overcoming the ignorance and prejudice
A world inhabited by beings of understanding hearts
Not splintered between races, nations and colors
A clear knowledge shattering the myths
No superior, no inferior beings
Except the shine they contain
Reflecting the points of achievements
Exhibiting the extracts they retained
While treading the arc of evolution
Skill to master the lower self
Put to test again and again
The old vices hard die
Rising, bewildering anew
The magnetic pull downwards
Ever so potent
Ignoring the warnings and portent
From above the vision so clear
The old monsters raising their ugly heads
Devouring the self destructive fools
While darkness of ignorance reigns
The world, nearing its logical end

******

Consternation

The music not soft but like furious storm
Entered the consciousness and made me shiver
The harsh sound like rattling swords
Like stones rolling down the hill
Thunders roaring in clouds on height
Ready to cast thunderbolts
I shudder and do all
To hush the invading hums
To stop the beating drums
But the sound of music went on
In subtle realms beyond
As the recipient remains the soul
Soul thrives dancing on tunes
Body feels trapped in sand dunes
Fearing the worst to happen
Shivering with severe cold
In burning summer heat
Unable to know what went on
As a name or term is not given yet
To this state of mind

Comets

Out of nowhere they appear
Transpiring the limitless sky
All bright, with a long tail behind
But they are a temporary phenomenon
Passing, disappearing in unknown
As abrupt as their appearance
The real stars were and remained
An integral part of the heavens above

****

Circle around

Moon around Earth
Planets around Sun
Time around life
Life around Him
Where all begins
Where all ends
Each seeks path straight
But instead
Circles round and round
Hope to find the gate
All dashed to the ground
Yet resolve, a staunch warrior
Remains unshaken
The quest marches on

*****

Confusion

Raised to exploit, nurtured by greed
In times like these, the worlds' go blind
Chains of slaves, rattle in the air
Chase of dreams while truth lags behind

*****

Narcissist

The artist looked at his created piece
Was amazed by its contours clear
Astounding bright colors
Alluring, fine details
Captured his gaze
Enthralling, enchanting his heart
Filling it with pride
Was that another masterpiece
A crown of his creation?
Without a doubt it was, he was convinced
He wasn't even aware
That the created piece has been just a mirror
Reflecting, projecting
His hopes, wishes and grandiosity
Making him fall in love
With his own very self

Different reactions

A wizard once said
Reactions to wrongs and evil vary
The bravest would fight back
With all the might they possess
With all the tools available
Next to them would denounce and condemn
Loud and clear, so the world could know
What they stood for
Many would dare not to utter their thoughts
Just hating the evil within their feeble hearts
Cowards but still part and parcel of good
Beware the rest, he warned
They are wrong doers or ignorant
Very easy preys and tools in hands of evil

*****

Distance

If the moon were to enter
Into Earth's sphere,
No moon was to be left
Would it be worth an embrace?

Existence on Periphery

So long they had subsisted
With dangers ever looming
Overhead
The animals of prey
Adjusted to realities bitter
Dashed as fast as they could
Each time the lurking threats neared
Always perplexed
At the swiftness of events
Claws of destiny
Grabbing in the moment of neglect
The knowledge lacking
Situations were provisional
Period but transitory
Dangers enduring
The predators weren't to be satisfied
Nature wasn't to be pacified
By occasional feast of prey few
The noose around existence tightening
The pain enhancing, the tensions heightening
They remained indulged in frivolities

Extract

Trust and faith are colors sharp
Strife and purpose pillars of life
A heavenly home or living hell
A pair of choices with a wife

****

Heartbreak

Emotions arise from the center so strange
Ripples turning into stormy waves
Earthquakes of great magnitude
Epicenter so close to the heart
Shock waves after shock waves
Disturbing the rhythm of life
Each drop of blood
All drenched in grief
Leaves the invisible track
Behind
Sorrows all piled up
Weigh heavy
Strain the heart
Wear and tear's process
Sets in
Taking the joy of life
The more a heart takes heat
The wiser gets the soul

Golden Fingers

Everything they touch
Into gold it turns
The wizards of crazy times
Inheritors true of Midas
Love their affluent lives
Unaware that all ultimately
Is doomed to come to an end
The moment not far
When the golden fingers
Would come in touch
With all those they love

*****

Metamorphosis

Bonded energy is matter
When destroyed again energy
Appearance and disappearance
Games divine
All eternal, nothing destructible
Why the human life
Should be an exception?

Heart without love

A heart without love is
A tree without fruit
A fruit without taste
A flower without fragrance
A lamp without oil
A bird without wings

A heart without love is
A river all dried out
An ocean without depth
A cloud all drenched
A sun without heat
A star without glitter

A heart filled with love
Burns and cause pain
Demanding endurance, sacrifice
Inflicting sufferings n insults
Drenching all energies pure
Breaks hearts without a cure
And yet its presence
A great blessing
Inevitable
For a purposeful life

No blame on Moon

The sun shone in all his glory
Spreading the rays of power
The golden beams
Penetrating, energizing
The worlds around
Illuminating, piercing the heart of darkness

Diana, deprived of her own shine
Felt the angst of insufficiency
A desire to stand in the limelight
Creeping into her mind
She cried and wished
She too had something to give

Her cunning head
Presented a solution innovative
To stand and shine
Along with others in the sky
And have her head high

She absorbed the golden rays of the sun
And when the sun vanished from the horizon
She reflected, what wasn't hers
The silver beams
Divorced from the warmth
Emptied of heat
But nevertheless she shone
With a broad smile on her face
All content and proud

Merciful life

Each blow, each injury
Enhanced the pain
The heart cried in indignation
Devastated, bitter and aggrieved
Frustration, overwhelming
A silent protest, a resentful cry
How life could be
So unjust, so very cruel

Wipe off the tears
See around without
The tears of self pity
Whispered someone
Doing that
Saw, the world around
With shock and awe
Never complained after
As the truth had dawned
Life was so merciful
So very kind to me

Life marches on

The will to be, burns
Seeking the fuels that sustain
Both visible n invisible
Expanding, excelling, in all cells
Giving rhythm and patterns to follow
Offering dreams concrete and hollow
With perpetual struggle to survive
It wanes with passage of time
Unable to burn on low flame
Unaware of rules of game
It dances on tunes of joy
Recedes inward with biting grief
Eternal and yet so brief

****

Let go!

The flowing waters give life
The static stink
Bury that that's all dead
However dear to heart
Keep just the fragrance
Colors sharp and sounds
Memories good or bad

Knowledge

Is ignorance a blessing or a curse?
It's both, said the sage
A blessing, when spares pain
A curse, when deprives envisage

****

Inspiration

Like the drops of dew
Inspirational moments are few
They come to enlighten the mind
Approaching us only to remind
With fires of creativity
We need to forge divinity
Into beautiful sharp sword
If we long for peace & accord
As only that shining sword
Can cut asunder the falsehood

Life essence (H2O)

Falls from sky, longs to go back home
A playful transformation from fluid to gas
Turning solid, giving cold fires
Back to liquid state
A magical dance of elements
Pour down comes
To bring the force of life
For land and shapes diverse
All springs forth and sustains
When balances
Between elements prevail
A wonderful reservoir of energy
A fuel for vehicles of life
A light in darkened nights
A power generated
To fulfill the desires varying
Containing therapeutic qualities
All these and still more
Hidden powers of water

Insanity (Burning cities)

Swaying between lucidity and insanity
Turmoil turning in false tranquility
Fears soothed by twisted beliefs
Rationality drowned in excitement of expected
rewards
The gaze turned to swarthy spots
Where wind of hatred sweeps
A world so unreal, so distorted
Awaits the victims unaware
Children imprudent
Belonging to misguided ranks
Not knowing that grounds beneath their feet
Exhale the fumes of intoxication
Bending their tiny wills
To extent of suffocation
Exposing them to psychosis
A realm from where they can proceed
Without guilt or conscience
And take the lives of those around
Sending terror waves
Living hell appears for innocents
Rain of coins for few

****

Pieces of peace

No one can say for sure
If it was a grin
Or a sob out of despair
But certainly he did
Turn and turn in his grave
Grave number 170
Just outside Stockholm
When the Eagle landed
In Oslo

****

Imminent dangers

It smells appalling it looks bad
As the world takes a precarious turn
The forces of nature stand array
Simple truth none wants to learn

*****

Perfect harmony

In nature, exists not any equilibrium
Of permanent nature
States of harmony lack
But brief and fleeting
Forcing every single cell
To strive for something better
Content minds, permanent harmonic states
Close the doors of developments
Cease the activities dynamic

*****

Pandora's Box

The periodical box being opened
Filled up to the brim
With wrath of gods
Miseries, unhappiness, calamities
Swarm around in frenzy dance
Vengeance wears the color red
When the worlds' sink in gloom
All defeated, all perplexed
Spes, this time failed to save
Refrained from putting hope
A tragic drama begins
Where gods laugh and laugh

Science of advertisement

Sensuous sounds employed
In order to seduce
Colors of spectrum
Being chosen with care
Images that incite the mind
To wrestle with temptations strong
Blindfolded jumps sanity
In the hells of matter
Seeking the compensation
For not knowing
The dweller within
Thus the process of piling up continues
Surrounded by soulless gadgets
The sad journey continues
On lonely trails of existence

*****

Recognition

Listen to the moans and cries
Begging for relief, for interference
Watch the eyes of the distressed
Exhibiting pain and despair
Feel the sorrows of those around
Struggling to stay alive
Who could anticipate
Starvation in days of abundance
The watchful eyes of prudent
See the signs so clear
Sensing the hour promised
Tearful, humble they fear
Each holding his faith so tight
Yearning for the glorious light
Not knowing
The temples, synagogues, the churches
Stood emptied from spirit divine
They no longer hold the shine
Of one living God
Shun the old that's adulterated
Let go that what's doomed
Stand free from impervious beliefs
As they'll just hinder
From bowing to truths revealed
The knowledge, the certainty
Wouldn't be enough
Again and again
The truth has been rejected
By those awaiting
Unable to recognize
New not corresponding, compliant to old

Resurrection

Death needs to be tasted
Before new birth can take place
For new to come and proclaim
The old has to crumble, give way
Surrenders' heartbreaking
Freedoms hard to obtain
Forms wither
Dust to dust
Ashes to ashes
Dogmas not easy to pass away
Keep minds in grip
Blocking the way to sway
The fierce resistance
A bigotry insistence
To be principles eternal
While in reality
Just thought forms
A vague reminder of the truth
This blindness
Open the gates of hell
As the way to heavens
Passes through midst of hell
A man, his achievements have to die
Physically, metaphorically
Before resurrection can occur
New heaven n new Earth
Descend
Sphinx can be seen
Rising from the ashes

Solar eclipse

Sun needed a spouse
Earth not suitable choice
Too fertile, loaded with offspring
Getting close it would burn
Getting afar, it would freeze
The fragile life on earth
Diana, the best possible pick
Barren, all available
To her, he courts
Every now and then
Making artificial dark
Rest of story
A mystery great

*****

Sodom & Gomorra

A sign, a symptom
Pronouncing the completion of a cycle
All the given goals achieved
The creative forces recede
Regeneration, recreation, losing the sting
Leaving behind the chaos and disorders
To sweep all around
Preparing the fiery battlegrounds
Where the Combat takes place
Exposure to fires of truth
Where stern evaluator stands unflinchingly
Sodom & Gomorra, the symbols of past
Remain arrogantly defying
Unaware that it was just a respite

****

Stars of Heavens

Had not been
The stars of heavens
So far stretched
Burning with heats incredible
Had not been
The hands of the race so tied up
The hearts, so feeble
The vault of heavens
Would certainly have been
Long emptied of its glowing stars
Given, sacrificed
On the altars of vain lovers
Hanging instead
From the firmaments
There would have been
Deep sighs
Gloomy lamentations
Of sad, depressed poets

****

Strange creatures

Beasts of the wild kill but to fill their bellies
An inborn instinct, a mean of survival
Calamities strike and take their toll
All in accordance with the law
The warlords bring the armies face to face
To kill and destroy the foes
A struggle to gain and dominion
To exhibit power and prominence
A strange creature is man
Who can slaughter and ravage for nothing
A destructive force
A mass killer
One has to traverse the universe
To find a similar kind
Deprived of merciful hearts
Devoid of compassion and love
The maniac annihilate
All that comes their way
They kill but with ardor
They destroy but with conviction
Equipped with justifications
In their minds exist no contradictions
Land, ideology and twisted cause
Indoctrination, frenzy and hate
Turn the imbeciles
In to living, ticking bombs
Capable to inflict suffering and pain
On mass scales
The muck of the earth
The monsters in disguise

Insane Times

Can be found in all lands
In all races and faiths
All those who disregard
Human dignity and life
Kill the innocents, non combatants
Can be classified as terrorists
Regardless of if these brutes
Represent some misguided elite
Or wear the uniforms

****

Predator

The eagle hovered on heights great
Looking down at the valley below
Searching for the prey with his piercing ocular
Eager to find and devour
The flesh of Raptors unaware

The eagle circled, measured and calculated
To enhance the chances of its success
To pinpoint the surface beneath
Before releasing the thunderbolts
Towards the hideouts of its preys

The valley shook and shivered
Of this sudden strike
Terrorizing the hearts that heard
The most terrible sounds
There lingered the smoke, dust and stank
Of burning flesh

The Iron eagle turned and retreated at ease
Spreading its wings, floating on the breeze
Towards its resting place
It had done for the day
The strange bird without a beak or a stomach
And yet kills indiscriminatingly and spread horror and
destruction
In the pre-dawn raids

Leaving behind
A shattered target
Scattered limbs
Smoky debris
Annoyed feelings, explosive rage
Multiplied numbers of those
Who were supposed to be destroyed
Along with the innocents

*****

Sun's labor

The Sun rises from the east
Saw west still drenched in dark
His heart sought to illuminate
By chasing darkness away
A Herculean labor starts
The glorious sun smiles
As his golden rays
Pierce the shadows dark
Smiting, forcing them to flee
It's not before the end of the day
The triumphant sun turns and sees
Darkness engulfing east
He rushes to pursue dark
Thus toils day and night

*****

Supreme Justice

Despite the promised reward of paradise
Not easy to subsist in conditions hostile
Evil rules Earth and holds the keys to bliss
What's left for good is just imagination fertile

Sunrays

Good morning!
Whispers a sunray
Kissing the sleeping bud
Here we're to fill you
With warmth and love
To make your bright colors visible
Reveal your stunning beauty
Give you strength to bloom
The bud's heart was touched
Filled with peace and joy
Sunrays kept falling
Penetrating in the bud
Sacrificing their lives
As the sacrifice remained the law
By which they abide
So that the bud could get
Heat and power
To display the beauty
By opening, revealing
Petal by petal
With an effort great
To show to the worlds around
What innocence could look like
By releasing its fragrance
Entrusting it to the gust
A message is sent
A secret is disclosed
Declaring loud and clear
That's my love for the one
Who created me

Take your time

A time appointed
From the conceiving to delivery
A period needed
From sowing
To the cultivation
A tree bears not fruit
All year around

Only the best of vines
Need ferment into wine
Then to mature
For time appointed
Till they can be enjoyed
To satisfaction complete

The thoughts thus need
A span to whirl around
In the midst of mind
Before they can be presented
As food for thoughts
In the world
Facing emergencies new
Where souls starve

Superiority Complex

Divisions, both external and within
A process determined to succeed
Through think and thin
Classes diverse, symbolic castes
Selective elite and masses gray
With intact order flourishes lands
With outspread chaos all decay
Equality in nature!
A far-fetched dream
A visible connection
Existing between
Upstream and downstream

Dominate or be dominated
Nothing in between
Duties assigned
All according to significance n competence
Yet the best of the whole
An ultimate goal
Smooth flow of energy
A prerequisite
A strategy of survival
Currents of life uniting
High to low
As above, so below
Divergence from law
Forces system's collapse
Superiority without wisdom
Leads to disasters great
Annihilation awaits

The axis of......

Never the same, moves from place to place
Self-preserving, equipped with intelligence sharp
Is the prince of dark
The spirit of great land, innocent, naïve
An easy prey to forces infernal
The cunning old hag
With a flicker in eyes
Won't let go
If not glory then shadow of power
She weaves the complots and smiles
The vibrant lies in holy mid
Where dark one sits and have his dream
To rule the world at large

*****

The Buzz

Crowds were to shout of excitement
If God was to be visible on the firmament
Just a few weeks and they would be bored
Finding no thrill if the change permanent

The co-creators

Ample resources
Available ingredients
Given forms and designs
An incredible, creative force
An inquisitive mind
Powerful currents of ambition
An unabated hunger
An unquenched thirst
To be and prevail
Dreams to be recognized
Tools marvelous devised
To carve the way of success
And yet the co-creators
Couldn't become anything more
But masters of recreation

****

The Imperfect senses

Our tools to learn and explore
Leading to hall of perception
Capable to raise us to the heavens
Or drag us to quagmire of deception

******

The Poets

We aren't no kings, who wear the silken robes
Neither do we play on the golden harps
Nor have we wealth and might
In search of bare sustenance
We turn to left and right
But we know the art to play
On strings of our humble hearts

The question of faith

In the midst of miseries
The faces of staunched
Kept glowing
With tranquility and peace
Strengthen by their faith
Anchored in belief
Looking at the empty hole
Deep in the soul
I sighed
Why?
I wondered
The lamp of faith
Shines not
Illuminating the inner realms
Dissipating the darkness around
Giving the gifts of trust and belief
Heart shed a bleeding tear
The mind laughed mockingly
Reminding me the day
When I had sacrificed
Faith on altar of my
Prudent but proud Intellect

Throes

When twinge surpasses limits bearable
Place attention to mind numb
Beyond the realm of pain exists the incredible
Enlightenment lurks in dimensions dumb

***

Turbulence

As the situation unfolds
New techniques are devised
To control and imprison
The weak, the meek
Sky high is misery
Cheaper gets life
The destiny of nation, the world
Rests in hands corrupt
A silence reigns
In deafening sounds
Power stays
With selective few
The shake of Earth
Seeing cataclysm approaching
While greed prevails
In hearts fraudulent

UFO

Aliens from the outer space
Trying to get in touch
Beings from inner sphere
Trying to get attention
We remain, but focused
To desires vain
Unable to peep down
Incapable to see beyond the stars
Where advance life forms
Await in anticipation
The day the humanity
Will finally break the law of gravity
Soar like Horus
****

Upside down

Their Lord supreme told to men
Satan was their adversary eternal
Seeking their fall from places esteemed
Inciting them to commit crimes
Seek protection from thy Lord
Against devil and his kind
From pious came a constant reminder
But one day something strange occurred
I heard a heartbreaking cry
A distressed prayer
A fearful plea
Satan seeking refuge from the Lord
Against the evil of men

Speedy mind

What a journey!
From bull-carts
To speedy jets
All in a twinkling of a century
Eye of vision bewildered
Incapable to grasp
The day, speed of light
Would look like
Crawling of a creep
When the energy of thoughts
Would soar around
Trafficking the universe

*****

A measuring Stick

Gone are the days, when people were handicapped
and confused
At the diversity of available tools
To measure things around
The old system was time consuming, knowledge
requiring
 But most of all inefficient
Necessitating common standardization
Requiring an instrument exquisite, a device unique
Putting an end to all existing mechanisms and tools

All one had to do was, to place the magical weight on
one side of the scales
And it could measure anything on the other side of
the scales

The great juggler had finally succeeded in inventing
the gadget
The new powerful tool was capable to gauge all and
everything

It could measure gold, silver or evaluate the precious
stones
It could determine even the price tag for misery and
pain
Or dignity of the rich
The commodities, weighed on its incredible scales
Could get the equivalent rates
The values of properties could be determined
Every single item could be computed

A measure more precious, precise and trustworthy
Than anything the world had ever known
 The Diamonds could crumble and become dust
But not the new instrument
Was declared by the wizards of the race

That wondrous measuring stick prevails
Dominating the entire world
Serves the race of men
The race of men
Holds it close to its heart
One measures not only the material worlds with this
astounding tool
But even the things vague, abstract and subtle
No longer need for ethics, values or the spiritual
strength
The new tool is strong enough, all pervading
Can judge and take care of all

That was and still is, a magic stick
Through which the worlds could be
Designed, build and sustained

From that time on
All the talents could be evaluated
Without the flinch of doubt
All stories of failures or successes
Could be read loud and clear
The division of respectable and disrespectable
Was so obvious and true
The new tool could measure not only
The character, properties but even the depths of one's
soul
It was worth living, striving for

Even worth dying for
The new precious measuring stick
That bewilders the bewitched humanity
Is nothing else than the magical
Almighty Dollar
With which the world ever since
Is being driven by

*****

A World of your own

At times when the pressures of the world become
unbearable
The attack of storming distress engulfs and consumes
me completely
The heartbeat of the time deafens the ears
As it sounds more like explosions taking place
Shaking, threatening my whole existence
Leaving me without the defenses, depriving me of the
power of resistance

At times when the gloomy dispositions are all that I'm
left with
To deal with my sorrows, my bitter realities and
defeats
The times when the calamities lurk just around the
corner
And the loneliness takes me in her merciless clutches
I just smile and take the refuge, in something which is
huge
Against the mighty deluge

I unlock the door and enter in the world of my own
A world, which's trouble free
A friendly, soothing place
Where the anxieties can't penetrate
Where I can relax with certainty and never hesitate
A world free of all the dogmas, prejudice and taboos

In that wonderful world of mine
It's me, who create, sustain or destroy
When the need is no more
Thus the characters and scenes emerge and vanish
Just like the world outside

The difference between these worlds remains vast
In the outer world, I remain helpless, in the inner first
and last
The owner of a world, exclusively mine
The writer of the drama that enacts just in realms
unseen
The main character of the stories unique

****

BONDS

All relations, ties and emotional bindings have lives of
their own
Subject to ups and downs
Growing out of seeds unseen
Products of love pure, or fantasies unclean
May they be given or woven in the web of time
May they be loose or connections strong
To time alone do they belong
Like everything else in nature
They spring; they flourish, get weak, wither and die
Leaving us with a question
But why! Do the burning flames die?
Why the feelings get cold?
Why the affections worth gold, turn in to metals
worthless?
Why the living, loving hearts are prone, to become
that of stones?
Why the tenderness departs? Why the nurturing
hands fail?
Why the strong bonds weaken? Why faith in each
other crumbles?

Is it greed that consumes the healthy relations or is it
pride?
Oceans of wishes keep inflicting splits and divide
No gains are permanent, no losses are forever
And yet the treasures so precious, the achievements
so great
Relations so dear are sacrificed on the altar of
ignorance complete

But who is to be blamed?
All relations, ties and emotional bindings have lives of
their own
And a specific duration.
Remaining healthy and strong
As long as they fulfilled the function
Interacting, interweaving, and. growing cohesively
Arriving ultimately at the junction
From where they have to part
Say good-bye to the point achieved
And to proceed towards the challenges ahead
Careless of all, which is dead
So that the evolution could go on

*****

Credit Crunch

Trillions gone, trillions at the hold
Expansions hold depression's curse
Sooting promises, calming pills
The ailing patient seems to get worse

*****

Androgen

A life so rich, full of harmony
Before the division of Adam & Eve
Never ever found the other half again
The opposites just confront and leave

*****

Dusk

She looked at the sky and it reminded her something,
she had seen before
The struggle between the forces of light and dark
taking place
In the realms high above
This periodical thrashing about occurred every now
and then, she knew
Always resulting in the winning of one or the other,
never a tie
She knew a similar fight was going on deep inside
within her
The uncertainty, as to what was about to emerge was
scaring her to death
Shadows of anguish and fear lurked in her deep
worried eyes
Was the light to win the battle?
Giving her a glorious day
To shine in the inner space
Or was the darkness to overcome?
Pushing her to gloom and dismay
Her eyes gleamed of renewed hope
Seeing the forces of light gaining the ground inch by
inch
Piercing and dispersing the darkness with its arrows
of pure gold.
The dawn was heralding the glorious day
Her enthusiasm, her hopefulness and her confidence
knew no bounds
So absorbed was she by the outer reality that she
failed to give attention to what went on within
Where the forces of light were losing the ground
As it was dusk and not dawn as she had wished and

hoped for
Her strength and energies were waning rapidly

Leaving her at the mercy of forces dark
In the clutches of miseries and fogy deceptions
She was in a desperate need of some artificial
substitute light
In order to make the night of her life, liveable,
endurable
Before she fell into slumber
Never knowing with certainty, if she was ever to re-
emerge from that night of her life

****

East & West

From aeons to aeons
West is brought
 Face to face east
To learn the lessons due
Before usher the ages new
Each time west remains
Blind to the truth
Seeking gains and exploits
An unlimited expand
An unjustifiable, complete control
As it insists to stay
Too materialistic, too greedy
Negligent to spirit needy

East, a slumbering indolent
Hides in sanctuaries false
Refusing to press ahead
Blaming all on fate
Surrendering to glamorous gleam
Commuting between the extremes
While west, driven by ambitions blind

Trusting, just the cold light of mind
Keeps distancing, drifting
Further and further away
From that that bestows
Exonerating understanding
Thus east & west
Inch by inch
Moment by moment
Get closer to the seat

Where no intercessors are availed
Where truth shall prevail
Judgements shall be passed
The facts shall be revealed
As to where did they err

****

Encircled

In the center of the circle I stand.
Withholding the pressures extreme
Mixing the pain with joy
Comprehending the reality with a dream
For the midway traveler I am.

It's not fear, but repulsion that restrains me from
certain deeds.
Even though I know that actions are the seeds.

It's the impulse that leads my chosen steps
I push forward always fearing none.
Without seeking any reward.
Opting the way hard

For the failure or success of my eternal strife.
Is in itself, a bitter fruit of labor in vain
Or a reward Supreme

Falsehood

Nations get born, nations do die
Nations rise to power and glory
Intoxicated and blind with pride
They decay and destroy themselves
Becoming the part of the history
Even the gods arise
From some misty fog
Conceived by imagination fertile
They grow stronger
Fed by the faith and devotion
Their divine food
They demand, they enchain
They completely dominate
But even they have a short life
That comes to an end
When devotees turn their gazes away
The Olympian gods fell
And so did the Pantheon

All unreal has to vanish
Not able to stand the truth
Falsehood has a day to shine
With its black swarthy rays
Fill the hearts with love
Try to be fair and just
Wait with a hopeful anticipation
For the glorious day that comes

Time to give back

All the life he had remained at the receiving end
Finding himself on the mercy of others, his parents,
his kin and the society
They bestowed on him the gifts of all kinds
Molding, shaping and making him that what he
ultimately became
A man detached and divorced from his real self
All the meanness, all the insults, which inflicted on his
soul
All the deprivation and humiliations, which were
imposed on him
By those he revered, loved and cared for
But he remained thankful, subservient and enduring
Without a flinch or complaint
He felt that times had slowly changed
The crawling at the arc of evolution had brought him
to the point
A position, from where he could give back, the way
he found it fit

The time for retribution was in
The occasion he'd been waiting so fervently
But his inner refused to bow to the burning desire for
vengeance
So he decided to reward all the wickedness, all the
unkindness
All the insults, all the humiliations
All the wounds, all the austerities

Which were ever inflicted on his body and soul
The unfailing reward, which no one could ever hope
and expect of him
He had forgiven them every single crime, every single
atrocity
Which they had ever committed against him
And gave them the abiding treasures of love
In shapes diverse
If they were capable to profit from them or not, was a
thing to be seen

****

Universal Famine

The winds carried the clouds dark
To directions unknown
The dry, barren land below
Licked its dusty lips
Hoping the rain to fall

The clouds weren't touched
By the yearning heart
Of the land dying of thirst
Once fertile, now becoming sterile
The dance of joy
The whirling dust
Died down

The rays invisible
Penetrating the atmosphere
Were felt by the starving men
Who saw the ray of hope
In hopeful anticipation, they rejoiced

The rays touched the atmosphere and retreated
Bouncing back to directions anew
There was a cry of indignation
That turned into gloom and despair
And ached the longing hearts

It seemed
Famine of man was to continue
In all quarters of the world

As the blessing of the rain
Of light and energy potent
Was to stay all absent
At least for a while

Life is a never ending drama and so is the flow of the
poetry, so there is more to come from me.